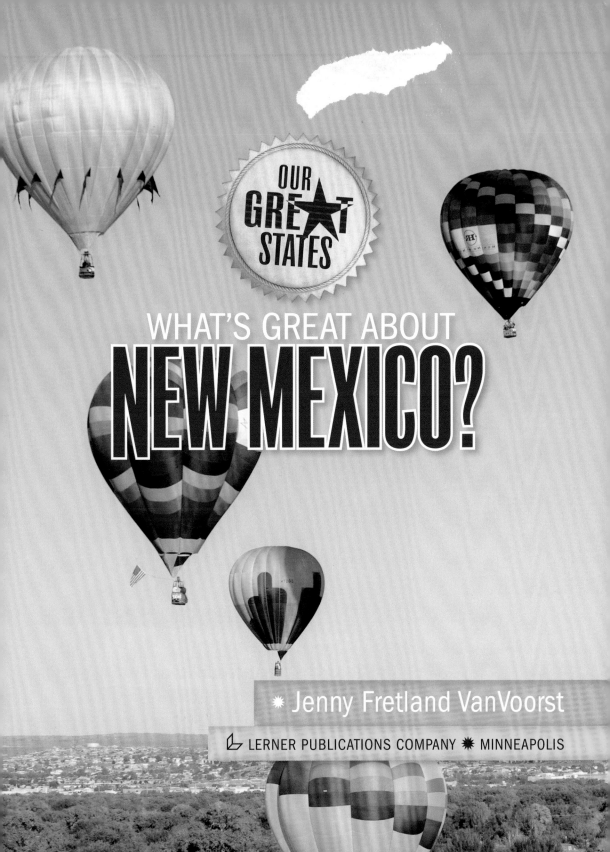

OUR
GREAT
STATES

WHAT'S GREAT ABOUT
NEW MEXICO?

✳ Jenny Fretland VanVoorst

LERNER PUBLICATIONS COMPANY ✳ MINNEAPOLIS

CONTENTS

NEW MEXICO
WELCOMES YOU! ✳ 4

Content Consultant: Rob Martinez, Office of
the State Historian, Assistant State Historian

Lerner Publications Company
A division of Lerner Publishing Group, Inc.
241 First Avenue North
Minneapolis, MN 55401 USA

For reading levels and more information, look
up this title at www.lernerbooks.com.

Main body text set in ITC Franklin Gothic Std
Book Condensed 12/15.
Typeface provided by Adobe Systems.

Library of Congress Cataloging-in-Publication
Data

Fretland VanVoorst, Jenny, 1972–
      What's great about New Mexico? / by
Jenny Fretland VanVoorst.
          pages   cm. — (Our great states)
      Includes index.
      ISBN 978–1–4677–3347–2 (library
binding : alkaline paper)
      ISBN 978–1–4677–4713–4 (eBook)
      1. New Mexico—Juvenile literature.
   I. Title.
F796.3.F75 2015
978.9—dc23   2014001998

Manufactured in the United States of America
1 - PC – 7/15/14

New Mexico Welcomes You!

If you're planning to visit New Mexico, prepare to be charmed. This southwestern state is full of beauty. You can go sledding down dunes at White Sands. Or you may want to explore American Indian culture at Chaco Culture or Four Corners. Stop and explore ghost towns, such as Lincoln. Visit the busy city of Santa Fe to see modern art and ancient artifacts. There is something for everyone in New Mexico. Read on to discover ten things that make New Mexico great!

Explore New Mexico's cities and all the places in between! Just turn the page to find out about the LAND OF ENCHANTMENT. >

Welcome to
NEW MEXICO
The Land of Enchantment

Wheeler Peak
(13,161 feet/4,011 m)

ROCKY MOUNTAINS

BLACK RANGE

OKLAHOMA

ARIZONA

TEXAS

MEXICO

USA
MEXICO

Rio Grande

Pecos River

Gila River

Farmington

Chaco Culture National
Historical Park

Rio
Rancho

Albuquerque

South
Valley

Santa Fe

Clovis

Lincoln

Roswell

Alamogordo

Hobbs

Carlsbad

Carlsbad Caverns
National Park

Las Cruces

N

Miles
0   20   40
0   20 40 60
Kilometers

The Balloon Fiesta ends each night with a fireworks show.

ALBUQUERQUE
INTERNATIONAL BALLOON FIESTA

> You don't want to miss a visit to Albuquerque. Ballooning fans gather for the Albuquerque International Balloon Fiesta. The world's largest collection of hot-air balloons stops here each year. The fiesta is one of the most photographed events in the world. Make sure to bring your camera! The pictures will be very colorful.

Arrive early in the morning to see the first hot-air balloons. About one dozen balloons from the Dawn Patrol take flight. The balloons light up the early morning sky. More balloons take flight about one hour later. Watch as more than five hundred colorful hot-air balloons fill the sky. Look for balloons shaped like owls, cows, or other unusual objects in the Special Shape Rodeo.

Find out how hot-air balloons work in the Balloon Discovery Center. You'll learn about the history of the sport and how to stay safe. End your day by taking a balloon ride!

A zebra is one of the shapes you may see during the Special Shape Rodeo.

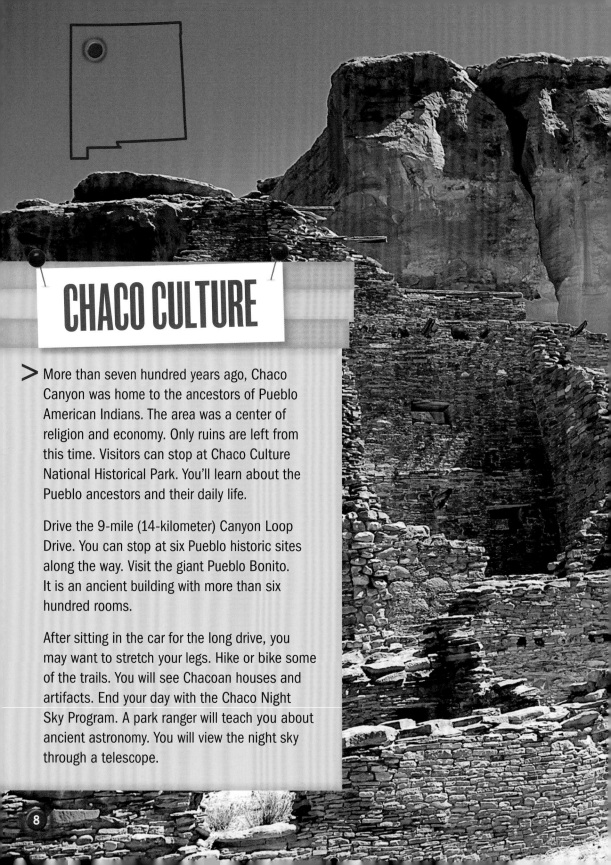

CHACO CULTURE

> More than seven hundred years ago, Chaco Canyon was home to the ancestors of Pueblo American Indians. The area was a center of religion and economy. Only ruins are left from this time. Visitors can stop at Chaco Culture National Historical Park. You'll learn about the Pueblo ancestors and their daily life.

Drive the 9-mile (14-kilometer) Canyon Loop Drive. You can stop at six Pueblo historic sites along the way. Visit the giant Pueblo Bonito. It is an ancient building with more than six hundred rooms.

After sitting in the car for the long drive, you may want to stretch your legs. Hike or bike some of the trails. You will see Chacoan houses and artifacts. End your day with the Chaco Night Sky Program. A park ranger will teach you about ancient astronomy. You will view the night sky through a telescope.

You may see ancient carvings in the rocks at Chaco Canyon.

AMERICAN INDIANS

Ancient artifacts teach us about earlier American Indian communities. But American Indian culture is still important in New Mexico. Twenty-two American Indian nations call New Mexico home: the Navajo Nation, two Apache nations, and nineteen Pueblo nations.

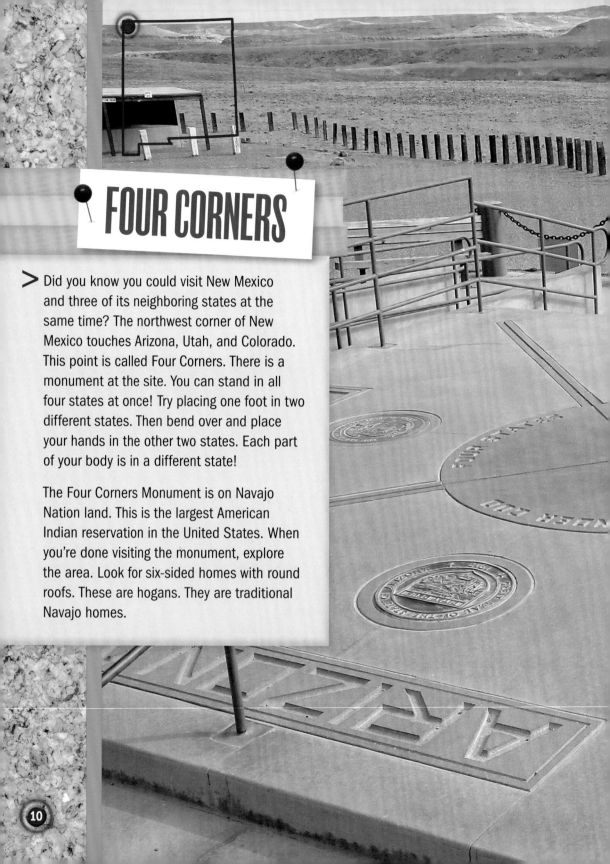

FOUR CORNERS

> Did you know you could visit New Mexico
and three of its neighboring states at the
same time? The northwest corner of New
Mexico touches Arizona, Utah, and Colorado.
This point is called Four Corners. There is a
monument at the site. You can stand in all
four states at once! Try placing one foot in two
different states. Then bend over and place
your hands in the other two states. Each part
of your body is in a different state!

The Four Corners Monument is on Navajo
Nation land. This is the largest American
Indian reservation in the United States. When
you're done visiting the monument, explore
the area. Look for six-sided homes with round
roofs. These are hogans. They are traditional
Navajo homes.

This is the only place in the United States where four states come together.

NAVAJO NATION

The Navajo Nation covers more than 27,000 square miles (69,930 square kilometers). It spans three states—Arizona, New Mexico, and Utah. Oil was discovered on this land in the early 1920s. Oil is a valuable resource that brings a great deal of money to the Navajo Nation. After finding the oil, the Navajo people decided to create a government. The Navajo government formed in 1923 and still exists.

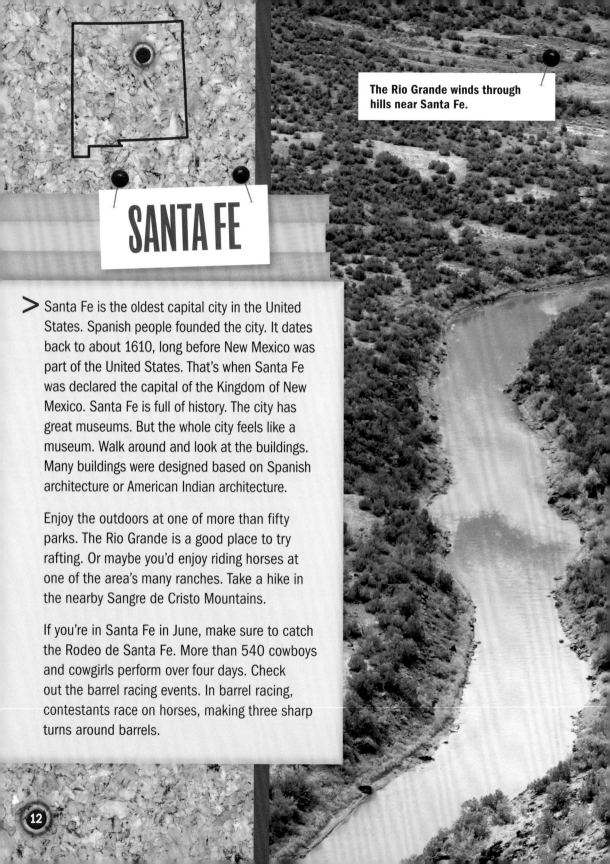

The Rio Grande winds through hills near Santa Fe.

SANTA FE

> Santa Fe is the oldest capital city in the United States. Spanish people founded the city. It dates back to about 1610, long before New Mexico was part of the United States. That's when Santa Fe was declared the capital of the Kingdom of New Mexico. Santa Fe is full of history. The city has great museums. But the whole city feels like a museum. Walk around and look at the buildings. Many buildings were designed based on Spanish architecture or American Indian architecture.

Enjoy the outdoors at one of more than fifty parks. The Rio Grande is a good place to try rafting. Or maybe you'd enjoy riding horses at one of the area's many ranches. Take a hike in the nearby Sangre de Cristo Mountains.

If you're in Santa Fe in June, make sure to catch the Rodeo de Santa Fe. More than 540 cowboys and cowgirls perform over four days. Check out the barrel racing events. In barrel racing, contestants race on horses, making three sharp turns around barrels.

Stop at the Rodeo de Santa Fe, which was founded in 1949.

Many buildings in Santa Fe look similar to ones the ancient Pueblo American Indians built.

THE GEORGIA O'KEEFFE MUSEUM

> New Mexico is known for its art. There are many art galleries, museums, festivals, and artists here. One of the best-known New Mexican artists is Georgia O'Keeffe. You can see more than one thousand of her works at the Georgia O'Keefe Museum in Santa Fe.

Walk through the exhibits and see O'Keeffe's famous paintings, drawings, and sculptures up close. The southwestern scenery inspired her work. You may see flowers, bones, rocks, and shells in her art. O'Keeffe often painted the same object many times. You may be able to spot the same flower painted different ways in a single painting.

Maybe you'd like to visit O'Keeffe's home and studio in nearby Abiquiu. Try taking a tour there. You will see how O'Keeffe lived and where she worked.

Georgia O'Keeffe found New Mexico's beauty inspiring.

Georgia O'Keeffe's home and studio are open for tours during part of the year.

This O'Keeffe painting is called "Red Hills with Pedernal, White Clouds."

LINCOLN

> Take a trip back in time when you visit Lincoln. It was once a ghost town, which means there were no people living in it. New Mexico is home to many towns where people no longer live. Lincoln is one of the most important. Start your visit at the Old Lincoln County Courthouse. Here, you will learn about the Lincoln County War. This was a fight for control of Lincoln that took place in 1878.

Continue your tour through the empty town. There are sixteen other buildings to see. Visit the Tunstall Store Museum. Goods from the 1800s still sit on the original shelves. You also can walk through a house, a tower, and a church.

If you visit in the summer, check out the Billy the Kid Pageant. You can learn more about outlaws and the Wild West.

BILLY THE KID

Many famous Wild West outlaws spent time in Lincoln. Billy the Kid (*right*) was a gunfighter, a thief, and an all-around bad guy. According to stories, by the time Billy died, he had killed twenty-one men. That was one man for each year of his life. Sheriff Pat Garrett shot Billy the Kid in 1881. Garrett later wrote a book about Billy's life. The book helped make Billy the Kid famous.

The Tunstall Store Museum still looks much as it did in the 1800s.

Billy the Kid escaped from the Old Lincoln County Courthouse in the 1800s.

17

ROSWELL

> Do you believe in unidentified flying objects (UFOs)? Some people do. Many people believe a flying saucer crashed in the desert near Roswell in 1947. Some say an alien body was found at the site. Walk through town to check out the many UFO-themed shops.

Visit the International UFO Museum. You will learn more about the Roswell crash. You also can learn about Area 51 and astronauts. Area 51 is a military base owned by the US government. It is unclear what happens at Area 51, so many people make up stories about it.

If you're visiting in July, stop by the Roswell UFO Festival. You will see alien costumes and hear people speak about UFOs. Thousands of people come to the event each year. End your day at the Area 51 Museum. You can take your picture with a fake alien.

The desert near Roswell is famous for the UFO crash that supposedly happened there.

The Roswell UFO Festival draws large crowds and creative costumes each year.

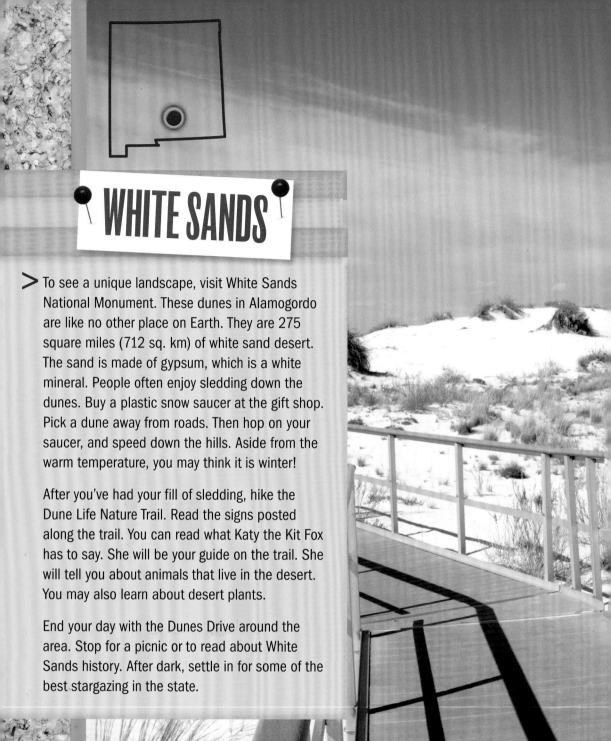

WHITE SANDS

> To see a unique landscape, visit White Sands National Monument. These dunes in Alamogordo are like no other place on Earth. They are 275 square miles (712 sq. km) of white sand desert. The sand is made of gypsum, which is a white mineral. People often enjoy sledding down the dunes. Buy a plastic snow saucer at the gift shop. Pick a dune away from roads. Then hop on your saucer, and speed down the hills. Aside from the warm temperature, you may think it is winter!

After you've had your fill of sledding, hike the Dune Life Nature Trail. Read the signs posted along the trail. You can read what Katy the Kit Fox has to say. She will be your guide on the trail. She will tell you about animals that live in the desert. You may also learn about desert plants.

End your day with the Dunes Drive around the area. Stop for a picnic or to read about White Sands history. After dark, settle in for some of the best stargazing in the state.

Sledding down the dunes is a popular and fun activity.

You'll learn about desert plants, such as the soaptree yucca, on the desert trail.

The entrance of Carlsbad Caverns is a winding, sloping trail.

CARLSBAD CAVERNS

> It's hard to imagine rooms the size of football fields underneath the desert. But this is what you'll find in Carlsbad. Carlsbad Caverns National Park is a system of 119 caves. And more caves are discovered all the time.

Some caves are harder to get to than others. You will decide how challenging you would like your tour to be. A park ranger will help you through your caving experience. Some cave tours take you to spots that are usually off-limits to visitors. You must wear a hard hat on other tours. You even may have to crawl through tight passages! The park ranger will point out cool cave features along the way.

There is plenty to do outside the caves as well. Hike above the park. Keep your eyes open for wildlife. You can watch the nightly bat flight. This happens from the end of May through late October. The bats leave their home in the caves to hunt for insects. They fly in a huge group.

FORMATIONS OF CARLSBAD CAVERNS

Carlsbad Caverns has amazing mineral deposits. Some look like swords covered in slime. Others look like diamond straws. The minerals form when water seeps into a cave. The water falls in little drops that contain small amounts of minerals. When the water dries, it leaves behind the minerals.

CHILE CAPITAL
OF THE WORLD

Members of Ballet Folklorico perform at the Hatch Chile Festival.

> If you like spicy food, you'll love eating in New Mexico. Spaniards brought chiles to New Mexico in the late 1600s. Southwest cooking often includes chiles. There are hundreds of kinds of chiles. Some are mild. You could eat one like an apple if you wanted. Others are so hot you'll feel like there's a fire in your mouth.

Hatch calls itself the green chile capital of the world. Each summer, the city holds the Hatch Chile Festival in honor of the green chile. Maybe you'd like to join the chile-eating contest. Or you can enjoy live music and games. Check out the Chile Cook-Off. Who can make the best chile recipe? Taste for yourself! Make sure to stop and watch the all-terrain vehicle (ATV) rodeo. People race on ATVs. The Chile Queen is crowned at the end of the festival.

Some chefs at the Hatch Chile Festival roast the chiles for people to try.

YOUR TOP TEN!

Now that you've read about ten awesome things to see and do in New Mexico, think about the places your top ten list would include. What would you like to see if you visited the state? What would you like to do there? These are all questions to consider as you make your own top ten list. Make your list on a sheet of paper. If you'd like, you can turn your list into a book. Illustrate it with drawings or with pictures from the Internet or magazines.

NEW MEXICO BY MAP

> MAP KEY

- ⬢ Capital city
- ◯ City
- ◯ Point of interest
- ▲ Highest elevation
- —··— International border
- —·— State border

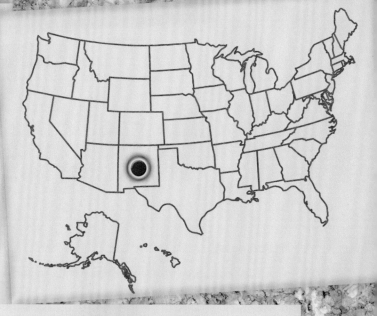

Visit www.lerneresource.com to learn more about the state flag of New Mexico.

26

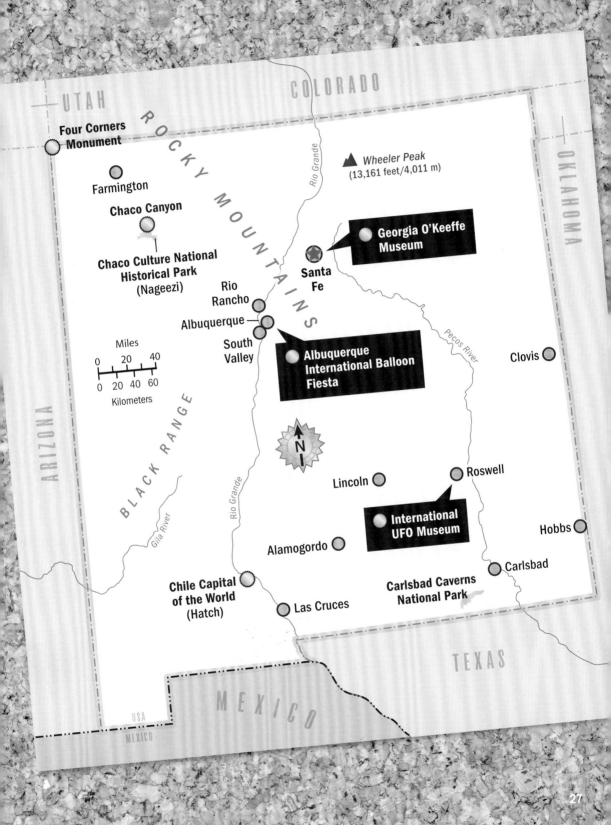

UTAH

COLORADO

OKLAHOMA

ARIZONA

Four Corners Monument

Farmington

Chaco Canyon

ROCKY MOUNTAINS

Rio Grande

▲ Wheeler Peak
(13,161 feet/4,011 m)

Chaco Culture National Historical Park (Nageezi)

Georgia O'Keeffe Museum

Santa Fe

Rio Rancho

Albuquerque

South Valley

Miles
0   20   40

0   20   40   60
Kilometers

Pecos River

Clovis

Albuquerque International Balloon Fiesta

BLACK RANGE

N

Gila River

Rio Grande

Lincoln

Roswell

International UFO Museum

Hobbs

Alamogordo

Carlsbad

Chile Capital of the World (Hatch)

Las Cruces

Carlsbad Caverns National Park

TEXAS

MEXICO

USA
MEXICO

NEW MEXICO FACTS

NICKNAME: Land of Enchantment

SONG: "O, Fair New Mexico" by Elizabeth Garrett

MOTTO: *Crescit eundo*, or "It Grows as It Goes"

> FLOWER: yucca

TREE: piñon

BIRD: greater roadrunner

> ANIMALS: black bear, New Mexico spadefoot toad, whiptail

FOODS: bizcochito, chiles, pinto beans

DATE AND RANK OF STATEHOOD: January 6, 1912; the 47th state

CAPITAL: Santa Fe

AREA: 121,593 square miles (314,924 sq. km)

AVERAGE JANUARY TEMPERATURE: 34°F (1°C)

AVERAGE JULY TEMPERATURE: 74°F (23°C)

POPULATION AND RANK: 2,085,538; 36th (2012)

MAJOR CITIES AND POPULATIONS: Albuquerque (555,417), Las Cruces (101,047), Rio Rancho (90,818), Santa Fe (69,204), Roswell (48,477)

NUMBER OF US CONGRESS MEMBERS: 3 representatives, 2 senators

NUMBER OF ELECTORAL VOTES: 5

> NATURAL RESOURCES: coal, crude oil, minerals, natural gas, solar and wind energy

AGRICULTURAL PRODUCTS: cattle, chiles, dairy products, hay

MANUFACTURED GOODS: electrical equipment, clay, glass, and stone products

> STATE HOLIDAYS OR CELEBRATIONS: Albuquerque International Balloon Fiesta

GLOSSARY

ancestor: a person who lived in the past

astronomy: the science of stars and other objects in space

culture: the beliefs, practices, and characteristics of a group

dune: a hill of sand piled up by the wind

exhibit: an article or collection in a museum

festival: a celebration in honor of a special occasion

inspire: to cause thoughts or feelings about a subject

mineral: a naturally occurring substance from the ground

outlaw: a criminal who runs away from the law

pageant: entertainment with scenes from history

reservation: an area of public land set aside for special use

telescope: a tubular instrument for viewing distant objects

UFO: unidentified flying object, or an object in the sky believed to be from another planet

FURTHER INFORMATION

Burgan, Michael. *New Mexico*. New York: Scholastic, 2012. This book offers a great deal of information about New Mexico in a fun, travel-guide format.

Lasky, Kathryn. *Georgia Rises: A Day in the Life of Georgia O'Keeffe*. New York: Farrar, Straus and Giroux, 2009. Check out this book for interesting facts about the great painter Georgia O'Keeffe.

McDaniel, Melissa, Ettagale Blauer, and Jason Lauré. *New Mexico*. Tarrytown, NY: Marshall Cavendish Benchmark, 2008. This thorough guide explores New Mexico's commerce, culture, geography, and history.

Nelson, Vaunda Micheaux. *Bad News for Outlaws: The Remarkable Life of Bass Reeves, Deputy U.S. Marshall*. Minneapolis: Carolrhoda Books, 2009. Read about Bass Reeves and his adventures tracking down criminals in the area that would later become New Mexico.

New Mexico Secretary of State Kid's Corner
http://www.sos.state.nm.us/Kids_Corner
This site offers a kid-oriented look at New Mexico's culture, geography, government, and history.

New Mexico—State Facts for Students from the US Census Bureau
http://www.census.gov/schools/facts/new_mexico.html
This site offers current, kid-friendly US Census data.

New Mexico Tourism and Travel
http://www.newmexico.org/?gclid=CIb8gcyar7oCFQcSMwod1nUAgA
Visit this site for up-to-date information about New Mexico's tourist attractions.

INDEX

PHOTO ACKNOWLEDGMENTS

The images in this book are used with the permission of: © Melissa Madia/Shutterstock Images, p. 1; © benkrut/iStockphoto, p. 4; © Laura Westlund/Independent Picture Service, pp. 5 (top), 27; © xyno/iStockphoto, p. 5 (bottom); © iStockphoto/Thinkstock, pp. 6–7, 13 (bottom); © Piyato/Shutterstock Images, p. 6; © icholakov/iStockphoto, p. 7; © BLFink/iStockphoto, pp. 8–9; © Steven Belanger/Shutterstock Images, p. 9 (top); © stellgp/iStockphoto, p. 9 (bottom); © Dr. Alan Lipkin/Shutterstock Images, pp. 10–11; © Jeffrey M. Frank/Shutterstock Images, pp. 10 (top), 20–21; © Autumn's Memories/Shutterstock Images, p. 10 (bottom); © Davor Lovincic/Shutterstock Images, pp. 12–13; © Craig Aurness/Corbis/Glow Images, p. 13 (top); © akg-images/Newscom, pp. 14–15; Library of Congress, p. 14 (LC-USZ62-103712); National Park Service, p. 15; © Luc Novovitch/Danita Delimont Photography/Newscom, pp. 16–17; © The Print Collector/Glow Images, p. 16; © Sheryl Savas/Alamy, p. 17; © powerofforever/iStockphoto, pp. 18–19; © Elvis Fontenot/iStockphoto, p. 18; © Kathy Burns-Millyard/Shutterstock Images, p. 19; © IrinaK/Shutterstock Images, p. 21 (top), 21 (bottom); © mtcurado/iStockphoto, pp. 22–23; © Name_Thats_Not_Taken/iStockphoto, p. 22; © Travelographer/iStockphoto, p. 23; © Marilyn Haddrill/iStockphoto, pp. 24–25, 25; © Catherine Karnow/Corbis, p. 24; © nicoolay/iStockphoto, p. 26; © graphmaster/iStockphoto, p. 29 (top right); © sjulienphoto/iStockphoto, p. 29 (top left); © photosoup/iStockphoto, p. 29 (bottom right); © sdbower/iStockphoto, p. 29 (bottom left).

Cover: Cover: © Randy Wells/The Image Bank/Getty Images, (balloons); © Travel Images/UIG/Getty Images, (parking); © Caitlin_Mirra/iStock/Thinkstock, (Chaco Canyon); © Laura Westlund/Independent Picture Service (map); © iStockphoto.com/fpm (seal); © iStockphoto.com/vicm (pushpins); © iStockphoto.com/benz190 (corkboard).